T0105001

THE BREAD
OF THE
SERVANT

An Easter Play in Four Acts

ELIZABETH G. HONAKER

WESTBOW
PRESS
A DIVISION OF THOMAS NELSON

WestBow Press books may be ordered through booksellers or by contacting:

WestBow Press
A Division of Thomas Nelson
1663 Liberty Drive
Bloomington, IN 47403
www.westbowpress.com
1-(866) 928-1240

Because of the dynamic nature of the Internet, any Web addresses or links contained in this book may have changed since publication and may no longer be valid. The views expressed in this work are solely those of the author and do not necessarily reflect the views of the publisher, and the publisher hereby disclaims any responsibility for them.

Any people depicted in stock imagery provided by Thinkstock are models, and such images are being used for illustrative purposes only.

Certain stock imagery © Thinkstock.

The Holy Bible, New International Version®, NIV® Copyright © 1973, 1978, 1984, 2011 by Biblica, Inc.™ Used by permission. All rights reserved worldwide.

ISBN: 978-1-4497-1163-4 (sc)
ISBN: 978-1-4497-1162-7 (e)

Library of Congress Control Number: 2011920796

Printed in the United States of America

WestBow Press rev. date: 2/17/2011

Dedication

To my Lord and Savior, Jesus Christ, Who
gave me new life in the Spirit.

To my loving husband, Allen, who gave
me his love over forty years ago.

To my children, James and Christine,
who gave me cause to rejoice.

To the Wesley Grove Disciples, who gave life
to the words in this and other scripts.

Introduction

Background

The play you are about to read is the product of over three decades of church-based drama dedicated to witnessing to the power of the Risen Christ. In 1977, the pastor at Wesley Grove United Methodist Church in Hanover, Maryland, initiated a yearly tradition on Holy Thursday night: the re-creation of the Last Supper in front of the congregation assembled in the sanctuary. For thirteen years, thirteen men portrayed Jesus and His twelve apostles in Scripture reading, words, and actions. It was a very simple performance, with limited movement and bathrobe-style costumes.

In 1990, I was asked to become the director of this group, and we named ourselves the Wesley Grove Disciples. Convinced that it was time to balance out the solemn message of the Cross with the encouragement of the Resurrection, I incorporated a message from Mary Magdalene into the traditional script, where she recounted her joy at discovering that Jesus Christ had risen from the dead.

In 1992, the group allowed me to experiment with my own scripts, which included more of the last week of Christ's earthly ministry. Then in 1995, I wrote a script that followed one character in his first-century encounter with Jesus Christ, from His early ministry through His sacrifice, resurrection, and ascension to the Father. Several scripts ensued between that year's offering and the script in this volume. They were all beneficial to actors and audience alike, but I chose this particular script to offer to you and other dramatists, first because it is my personal favorite, and because the Disciples performed it in both 1998 and 2008—a span of ten years. Between those years, the actors grew and developed enormously in their Christian witness, and the performances in 2008 were even more moving than those of 1998. It is to honor the depth of their commitment that I offer this script to a wider audience.

Sacred Imagination

I believe it was C. S. Lewis who first urged the use of "sacred imagination" to explain the Gospel to a jaded world—a world that often uses drama and acting to engage in improper thoughts and deeds that would land them in trouble in the real world! However, Philippians 4: 8 urges the Christian to focus on "whatever is true,... noble,... right,... pure,... lovely,... admirable,... excellent, or praiseworthy." Through engaging the imagination of the individual, I believe that we have an opportunity to re-create the sacred, and to set apart people, places, words, and actions to glorify God through drama.

Scholars differ as to when John the Apostle actually wrote his Gospel. I have used sacred imagination to suggest that he was an old man, already imprisoned on Patmos, when he either wrote (or revised) his version of the life of Our Lord. I beg the indulgence of those Bible scholars among you who may question the timeline I use for dramatic effect.

Getting Started

Any drama group just starting out has a number of questions—besides the obvious one of which script to perform. Where and when will rehearsals take place? Where will the play or skit be performed? How often will the performances occur? How should the group recruit actors, and what age should they be? Can the group afford to make, buy, or rent scenery, props, and lighting? What types of costumes does the production need? Can anyone in the congregation sew, or would they be willing to instruct those who might offer to make costumes? Does anyone have expertise with stage makeup?

Professional Christian drama groups have explained how to wade through these sorts of details quite well. Suffice it to say that there *are* creative Christians around you, eager to use the dramatic and technical skills God has given them for the Lord's work. Ask the Lord to help you find them. Search with a helpful, supportive eye, looking for those people who may need a little bit of encouragement, but who will surprise you with real expertise and great dedication.

The beauty of a ready-made script is that it gives everyone in the cast something to say and to do to further the Gospel. Even those actors who portray "bad guys" (such as Pharisees and Judas Iscariot) serve a wonderful purpose in the realm of drama: they provide opportunities for the "good guys" to speak the Truth of the Gospel! The Disciples have a wonderful Christian brother who, year in and year out, has volunteered to be "Judas"—and does him well. He does this with a loving heart, ready to serve in an undesirable role because, as he has stated countless times, "Someone has to do the dirty work." It is that kind of foot-washing that makes any Christ-honoring drama possible.

Place and Time

There are difficulties in presenting drama in either a church sanctuary or fellowship hall. We are used to doing "sacred" things in those places—certainly not setting up lights or props, or donning costumes or stage makeup. However, if the church building—and especially the sanctuary—is a place set aside for us to encounter God, with all our sins, troubles, problems, and miseries, can we not use that same sanctuary to represent how Christ can save and transform us? I can testify that it can be done tastefully, with a minimum of disruption to normal worship activities, and can, at the same time, spiritually energize those members of the congregation who shoulder the acting and producing responsibilities.

Why choose to perform a play in a sanctuary? Beyond the obvious desire to perform a play during the morning or evening worship service, my own experience has been that fellowship halls are often multipurpose rooms with little or no conventional staging area, no real sound equipment beyond the standard amp-mike combination, and no adequate stage lighting. They are not always centrally located, and their entrances are often merely functional—rarely beautiful or inspiring. On the other hand, sanctuaries are often reached through welcoming main doors in the building; sanctuaries are usually tastefully furnished, often with lighting that, at the very least, can be used constructively with a "switch operator" (someone who merely turns on and off the lights for each scene or act). They often have multiple mikes, and even the smallest congregation can afford a standing or body mike for placement near the place where actors are directed to stand. Most sanctuaries have relatively comfortable seating and are arranged so that all eyes are directed toward a central area.

You will notice that I have retained the conventional stage directions ("stage left" is on the actor's left while *facing the audience*, and "stage right" is on his or her right), while giving some directions uniquely suited to a performance in a sanctuary or pulpit area. I have also included directions instructing the actors to proceed down the central aisle (or an appropriate side aisle) of the church. This serves to draw the audience, especially children, more into the drama. In Wesley Grove Church, there are two upper (or elevated) doors into the sanctuary, and two lower doors immediately in front of the communion rails. If you have similar types of entrances, use them creatively to introduce actors into scenes, to draw the audience's attention to one space while you set up another, and so forth.

Performance Rights

I offer this script (and others to follow) as material for drama groups to present excellent plays for the glory of God. If you are interested in learning more about procuring performance rights and extra scripts, as well as more detailed production notes, please contact me at efghonaker@gmail.com. You may also write me at:

Elizabeth G. Honaker
P. O. Box 373
Sparta, TN 38583

The Disciples have produced DVDs of both the 1998 and 2008 performances, which might be useful to you in demonstrating how the Disciples presented this play. These can be sent to you for a donation of $25 or more.

Production Notes

This play revolves around the sacred memories of an elder John, the disciple whom Jesus loved. The character of John the Elder remains onstage throughout the entire play, and therefore I placed him on an elevated platform stage left (which happened to be behind our communion rail and stage left of the pulpit when we performed at our home church). As he and the character Diana interact, the stage lights are focused only on him. As John the Elder's memories unfold and the audience is directed to the action he recalls, the stage lights dim on John the Elder and Diana and focus on the scenarios. In both instances, when the stage lights are not focused on particular characters, those characters either freeze or exit, as the script dictates.

A note about stage lighting for John the Elder: he gives important insight into each scenario he remembers. It is best not to light him (and Diana) from above, where his face might be cast in unpleasant shadows. In the same way, be careful when using a single sort of lighting from the front; that arrangement might not give the best illumination to his face, either.

Over the years that the Wesley Grove Disciples have been presenting these plays, our scenery has tended to become simpler. At the beginning of my service as director, we were blessed to have a brother in the Lord who was gifted in construction. He devised a mobile stage curtain arrangement, which we successfully erected and utilized in many different church settings. However, as key members of the stage crew aged, we realized that this sort of set design was a bit too much for us to transport and erect for an evening's presentation. Therefore, we constructed a set of versatile flats that can be easily erected and arranged in just about any configuration, and whose fronts can be quickly transformed by a painted backdrop or artfully-arranged piece of cloth.

The Disciples have accumulated a storage room full of props over the years—some constructed, some transformed from ordinary, everyday materials. Make sure that the props you use do not have a distinctive twenty-first century flavor; these may prove distracting to the audience. On the other hand, some articles (such as mugs without handles) could be transformed into Last Supper cups and hidden among bread, fruit, and cloths lying on the table. For years, the Disciples have used an ordinary, undecorated, white ceramic jug with which to pour the grape juice for this scene. The design of a certain prop should take into account its function in the play, how often and where it will be used, and its distance from the audience.

With respect to costumes, I would urge you to watch such films as *The Passion of the Christ, Jesus of Nazareth,* and *King of Kings.* Some of these costumes may look quite complicated, but overall, they demonstrate the effective use of earth-tone fabrics and layering. I know that color can be extremely important when designing the costume of a character; therefore, I would advise that characters who are flamboyant be given more colors to wear (perhaps even some that clash a little). The character of Jesus should be given a distinctive costume that does not resemble any other costume, in order to make a visual statement about Christ's uniqueness.

Concluding Remarks

The important thing about Christian drama is its *intention.* We want to glorify God in all we do; props and scenery, even acting, are all secondary to this purpose. I have watched, amazed, as technical difficulties and even less-than-perfect acting have all unfolded in a particular production, yet members of the audience have afterward remarked how touched they were by the presentation. Bathe everything in prayer and a humble spirit; that is an essential component of this type of Christian witness.

I want to thank my sweet husband of almost forty years, Allen, for his unfailing support. Without him, I may indeed have written this and other scripts, but I would have gone hungry, unwatered, and distracted throughout the whole process! It is a well-known fact among the Disciples that the director could not survive writing scripts into the wee small hours of the morning without one of Allen's famous chocolate milkshakes! I would also like to thank my son James and daughter Christine, both of whom contributed sweat equity to the years of Honaker drama. In addition, Christine has become quite an expert in applying stage makeup, thanks to Mom's commandeering her services year after year!

Members of the Wesley Grove Disciples are some of the dearest, most loyal Christians you could ever know, and so I dedicate this play to them, for their sacrifice and service to the Lord. If I dared to try to mention them all, I would undoubtedly neglect one or another person, so I will leave this as a general salute and continue to mention you by name before the Throne of Glory. God knows your service, and He will reward it.

I would love to hear feedback from you or your drama group about this play (and others I hope to publish in the future). Please do not hesitate to contact me.

In His service,
Elizabeth Golibart Honaker

Characters (in order of appearance):

JOHN THE ELDER, Jesus' apostle John as an old man on Patmos
DIANA, a slave in the house of Arius

LAZARUS of Bethany
MARY, his sister
MARTHA, Lazarus' other sister *

JESUS, Messiah to the Jews and Savior of the world
JUDAS, a disciple who betrays Jesus to His enemies
MATTHEW, one of the Twelve Disciples
PHILIP, one of the Twelve Disciples
ANDREW, one of the Twelve Disciples
JONATHAN, Andrew's nephew
PETER, one of the Twelve Disciples
YOUNG JOHN, John the Elder as he was sixty years in the past
JAMES, brother to John

MARY MAGDALENE, a disciple of Jesus
NATHANIEL, one of the Twelve Disciples
THOMAS, one of the Twelve Disciples
MOTHER MARY, the mother of Jesus
HELENA, a follower of Jesus
SALOME, mother of James and John

MAN WITH WATER JAR
AMOS
WOMAN #1 at the fire
WOMAN #2 at the fire
ROMAN SOLDIER

CAPTAIN of the Roman guard
SALINIUS
DEMETRIUS
ANGEL at the tomb of Christ

Silent Disciples:
JAMES bar ALPHEUS *
SIMON THE ZEALOT *
BARTHOLOMEW *

GUARDS of the Sanhedrin *

CROWD, WOMEN *

* These characters are not assigned any lines, but they are to react to events that happen on stage. If there are not enough actors in the company, Martha can be eliminated, and the ROMAN SOLDIER and GUARD consolidated into one character. Similarly, there need be only two members to make up the crowd.

Act I, Scene 1

Scripture references: Genesis 1:1, 3; Isaiah 9:2; Zechariah 3:8–9; John 1:1–5, 10–12

A room in a small house on the island of Patmos. There is a raised platform upstage left, on which stand a small table and bench that can seat two people. On the table there are first-century writing implements, scrolls, pieces of parchment, and a candle sitting upright in its stand. A Jewish prayer shawl is draped over the front of the communion rail downstage center.

The stage is dimly lit. An old man, JOHN THE ELDER, *makes his way slowly—almost painfully—down the center aisle. He softly chants Psalm 138 or 145 as he walks. When he reaches the stage, he walks to the prayer shawl and drapes it over his head. Facing the audience, he begins to pray aloud.*

JOHN THE ELDER: Lord, I thank you for allowing your servant, John, one more precious day in which to serve You. I know my time here is short, and I have so much to tell the world about Your Son.

Finishing his prayer, he removes the shawl and leaves it where he found it. He makes his way toward the platform, then moves up the steps. With a small, grateful sigh, he settles down upon the bench. He lights the candle; the light on stage increases as he does. Then he picks up one of the scrolls and begins to read thoughtfully, with awe in his voice.

JOHN THE ELDER: The scroll of Genesis says, "In the beginning, God created the heavens and the earth … and God said, 'Let there be light,' and there was light."

Inspired by what he has just read, JOHN THE ELDER *picks up a quill or other writing tool and begins to write on one of the pieces of parchment, saying the words aloud as he writes.*

JOHN THE ELDER: In the beginning was the Word, and the Word was with God, and the Word ... was ... God.

JOHN THE ELDER *puts his writing tool down, pausing briefly. He is totally enraptured by his vision of God's greatness. Picking up the tool once again, he writes, again speaking the words as he writes.*

JOHN THE ELDER: He was with God in the beginning. Through Him all things were made; without Him nothing was made that has been made.

JOHN THE ELDER *pauses again. This time he picks up a scroll lying on the table, unrolls it, and reads aloud.*

JOHN THE ELDER: The scroll of Isaiah says, "The people walking in darkness have seen a great light; on those living in the land of the shadow of death, *a light has dawned.*"

These last words are delivered with emphasis. Laying down the scroll, he picks up the candle and studies it for a moment.

JOHN THE ELDER: In Him was life, and that life was the light of men.

JOHN THE ELDER *writes what he has just said. Then he turns his attention once more to the candle. Standing, he picks it up as if he were illuminating something beyond his work space.*

JOHN THE ELDER: The light shines in the darkness, but the darkness has not understood it.

JOHN THE ELDER *sets the candle down on the table. Picking up another scroll, he reads from it.*

JOHN THE ELDER: The scroll of Zechariah says, "Listen, people! I am going to bring my servant, the Branch ... and I will remove the sin of this land in a single day."

Putting down the scroll, JOHN THE ELDER *sits and begins to write again, speaking the words as he writes.*

JOHN THE ELDER: He was in the world, and though the world was made through Him, the world did not recognize Him. He came to that which was His own, but His own did not receive Him. Yet to all who received Him, to those who believed in His name, he gave the right to become children of God.

DIANA *enters from downstage right and crosses to the steps leading up to John's platform. She is carrying a wooden plate with bread on it and a cup of water.*

DIANA *(matter-of-factly)*: Come, old John, it's time to eat. Hurry and finish your dinner quickly; I've got better things to do than wait on you.

JOHN THE ELDER *(with good humor, despite her ill treatment of him)*: So, it is suppertime already?

DIANA *(hands on her hips)*: If you wouldn't spend so much time writing your stupid books, you'd know how the day passes.

JOHN THE ELDER *(rises; makes his way slowly down the steps to receive the food, speaking as he goes)*: Diana, we all have so very little time. I must tell all I know about the Master before He calls me home.

DIANA *(irritated)*: Forget about escape, old man! The governor is not likely to pardon you anytime soon!

JOHN THE ELDER *(with a chuckle)*: I was not speaking of the governor's pardon. I was speaking of God's summons.

3

DIANA: The gods! Who cares about them?

JOHN THE ELDER *(patiently)*: Not *the gods*, Diana! One God—one *true* God!

DIANA *(sarcastically)*: True to *what?*

JOHN THE ELDER: Not "true to *what,*" Diana. True to *whom*—true to *Himself.*

DIANA: Now, listen, old man! I don't care how many gods there are—one or a thousand—they are all the same. Sadistic, they are. Always causing trouble for mankind. I don't bother them, and they leave me alone. A blood sacrifice now and then to keep them satisfied ...

JOHN THE ELDER *(smiling, he produces a crude cross from a pocket in his robe as if it were a precious thing)*: Have you seen what I keep with me at all times?

DIANA *(spitting toward it angrily)*: A curse on that wretched thing! Why did you make such a thing? My father died on a cross in Jerusalem sixty years ago because the Romans said he was a thief! *(spitting again and getting emotional)* A curse on their crosses! A curse on them!

JOHN THE ELDER *(quietly and directly)*: My Master was crucified on a Roman cross sixty years ago.

DIANA *(reacting in horror)*: And you keep that accursed thing with you?

JOHN THE ELDER *(holding the cross higher, remembering)*: My Master served His Master by sacrificing Himself on a cross.

DIANA *(hesitantly)*: Who was His Master?

JOHN THE ELDER: God the Father.

DIANA *(shocked; sarcastic)*: A god as a father? Impossible! Absurd! And why would a fatherly god order his servant to die?

JOHN THE ELDER *(goes back up the stairs to sit down; beckons DIANA to follow him)*: It is a very long story, Diana; too long for an old man to tell standing up. Will you sit with me awhile as I explain?

DIANA *(turns as if to go; takes a few steps)*: I have better things to do than listen to fables, old man!

JOHN THE ELDER *(authoritative, yet gentle)*: If you listen to fables, you will learn only morality. If you listen to the story—the true story—I have to tell you, you will learn *love*.

DIANA *(stops in her tracks, turns her head, and asks cautiously)*: Why are you here, old man? Why have they locked you away on Patmos like this?

JOHN THE ELDER: Because I dare to believe that love allowed itself to be nailed to a cross.

JOHN *resumes his seat at the table on the platform.* DIANA *walks slowly back to the steps, goes to the top, and sits down next to him.*

Lights fall to blackout on the platform.

Main stage is illuminated.

Act I, Scene 2

**Scripture references: Matthew 6:24, 11:28–
30, 16:26; Luke 16:13; John 11, 12:8**

It is sixty years prior to the previous scene. The setting is the house of
LAZARUS *in Bethany, a town very near Jerusalem. There is a table
upstage center with a pitcher, cups, and plates of food on it.* JESUS *is sitting
at the table, upstage right; all of His disciples, including* MATTHEW
and PETER, *sit scattered throughout the stage, surrounding* JESUS.
LAZARUS *and his sister* MARY *stand behind the table.* MARTHA
stands upstage right. JUDAS *stands downstage far left. Lights come up
on the stage.*

MARY *(concerned, trying to make* LAZARUS *sit down next to* JESUS*)*:
Perhaps you should not be standing so much, Lazarus, my brother. It
has been barely a week since Jesus called you back from the dead.

LAZARUS *(laughing)*: Mary, you worry too much! *(smiles)* Jesus,
tell her she worries too much! *(mischievously, turns to* MARY*)* I will
show you how strong I am!

LAZARUS *picks up* MARY *playfully; she squeals. All laugh, except*
JUDAS, *who is preoccupied with his own thoughts.* LAZARUS *puts*
MARY *down, and she stops in her tracks, having suddenly realized
something about* JESUS. *With a solemn, almost frightened look on her
face, she exits downstage right.*

LAZARUS *(calling after her)*: Mary! *(to the others)* Now what's gotten
into *her?*

Becoming more serious, LAZARUS *picks up the pitcher from the table
and pours liquid into a cup.*

LAZARUS: You have shown us God's great love through Your miracles, Master. Now tell us more about *serving* this wonderful Father God.

LAZARUS *hands* JESUS *the cup and sits down at the table.* JESUS *stands.*

JESUS *(looking around)*: A man cannot serve two masters. Either he will love the first and hate the second, or he will willingly serve the second one and show disrespect to the first one. Money and God, Lazarus—they are two very opposite masters.

JESUS *begins to make His way downstage right.* JUDAS *looks away from his Master, as though he were tired of* JESUS *talking and would like Him to stop.* MARY *reenters from downstage right, a perfume bottle in her hands. For a moment, she hesitates, looking at* JESUS. *Then suddenly, she kneels before* JESUS, *deliberately takes the top off of the bottle, and pours the contents lovingly on* JESUS' *feet. She wipes His feet with her veil. Everyone except* JUDAS *stays where they are, watching, amazed. Only* JESUS *does not look amazed.*

JUDAS: *(Coming from where he has been standing, he grabs the bottle from* MARY *and shakes it at her.)* Of all the stupid things to do! Why wasn't this perfume sold and the money given to the poor? It was worth a year's wages!

Seeing that the bottle is now empty, JUDAS *throws it to the ground, causing* MARY *to move hurriedly out of the way.* JESUS *reaches out to hold his arm.*

JESUS *(in a firm voice)*: Leave her alone! *(He picks up the bottle from the ground.)* This perfume has always been set aside for the day of My burial. *(He pauses as this sinks in to the spectators.)* Judas, you will always have the poor among you. Help them whenever you wish. But you will **not** always have **Me**.

JESUS *turns back and walks toward the table. Two members of the* CROWD *enter the room and go to where* JESUS *is, drawing His attention for the moment. While everyone's attention is absorbed with the newcomers,* MATTHEW *stands and takes* JUDAS' *arm, crossing with him downstage left as far as possible.*

MATTHEW *(in a conciliatory tone)***:** Peace, brother! Why did you get so angry with Mary?

JUDAS: *(Smarting, and angry with* JESUS *for the rebuke, he frees his arm from* MATTHEW'S *grasp.)* Did you **hear** how He rebuked me, Matthew?

MATTHEW *(good-naturedly)***:** What are you getting so angry about, Judas? The perfume belonged to Mary, didn't it? A woman is free to use her things as she sees fit! *(gesturing toward* LAZARUS*)* You don't see her **brother** getting upset, do you? Besides, a little perfume now and again *(he holds his nose and indicates all those around him)* makes life among us travelers much more pleasant, wouldn't you agree? *(He places his hand on* JUDAS' *shoulder, as if to steer him back to the group.)* Come, sit down, and be pleasant.

JUDAS *(once again shrugging free of* MATTHEW*)***:** You just don't **get** it, do you, Matthew? Haven't you an **ounce** of sense since you left your tax collector's table? Do you have **any** idea of the price of food in the marketplace? How are we going to pay for the Passover feast if we've no money?

MATTHEW *(suddenly becoming very serious, almost suspicious)***:** It's not about food prices, Judas! It's not about perfume, or Mary, or the poor! It's about honor and prestige—isn't it? It's about who's going to be on top when the Master is welcomed as the King of Israel! You want people to serve **your** interest. You would like everyone to be **your** servant!

JUDAS *(drawing his robe together in a dignified manner)***:** I only want to be recognized for what I've done for this group.

MATTHEW *(scoffing)*: Yeah! Right! *(He returns to his place at the table.)*

The members of the CROWD *who have been talking to* JESUS *stand aside for the next lines.*

JESUS *(raising His hands in prayer and facing the audience)*: I praise You, Father, Lord of all things, because You have hidden these things from the wise and the learned and revealed them to little children. *(looking around at everyone)* Come to Me, all you who are weary and burdened, and I will give you rest. Take my yoke upon you—the yoke of One Who serves—and learn how to do this from Me, for my heart is gentle and I walk humbly before My Father. My yoke is easy, and my burden is light.

JUDAS *(talking to himself)*: How can the yoke of poverty sit easily on my shoulders? How can I accept the burden of a Man Who does nothing to ease my misery?

JESUS *(having heard)*: Judas, I pose a question to you.

JUDAS *(sweetly and obediently)*: Ask whatever You will, Master.

JESUS *(directly and to the point, gazing intently at* JUDAS*)*: What does it profit a man if he gains the **whole world**, yet loses his connection with the Almighty One—his very soul?

JUDAS *(avoiding His gaze)*: I have no answer for that, Master.

JUDAS *exits abruptly, downstage left. All freeze. Lights fall to blackout on the main stage. Platform is illuminated.*

Act I, Scene 3

Scripture references: 1 John 3:16, 4:16–19

JOHN THE ELDER *and* DIANA *resume their conversation from Scene 1. Everyone except* JOHN THE ELDER *and* DIANA *exit quickly and quietly while Scene 3 unfolds.*

DIANA: But Judas was certainly right! Everyone needs to watch out for himself. I have no wish to stay poor if I can help it.

JOHN THE ELDER: Which is the greater poverty: to have no wealth, or to have wealth and no soul? Judas was indeed proud of his position as treasurer of our group—and that pride closed his soul to salvation.

DIANA *(standing)*: What is all this nonsense your Jesus spoke about yokes and burdens—about being a servant? I hate serving—I hate serving Rome, I hate serving my master, and I hate serving **you**! *(She points angrily to the plate and cup she brought earlier.)* So hurry up and finish, so I can finish my chores for the evening.

JOHN THE ELDER *(gently, thoughtfully)*: Are you hungry, Diana?

DIANA *(scoffing)*: What? *(pointing to his bread)* Are you offering me **that**? I've had better meals when I was a slave in Rome.

JOHN THE ELDER *(Standing, he reaches to touch her shoulder.)*: There is a kind of hunger in you that no earthly bread can take away. It is a hunger deep inside you.

DIANA *(pushing his hand away)*: How can you **possibly** know what is inside me?

JOHN THE ELDER: Jesus always knew what was in the heart of a person. He always saw the need. When I became His servant, I began to see the need in the hearts of other people. I see your need now.

DIANA *(contemptuously)*: You pompous fool! What makes you think *I* need anything?

JOHN THE ELDER: There is not one living soul who does not need true love—love that serves and love that saves.

DIANA *(very defensively)*: What do you mean by ***that***?

JOHN THE ELDER: Diana, even if you don't believe me, I must tell you that the Lord God Whom I serve has created us out of His love. He created us because He needed someone to love. And if the Lord of the universe needs to love humanity, I know without any doubt that we need to be loved ***by*** Him! We have a need to serve Him, even if we don't recognize that need. *(as a sort of confession)* You are right about one thing, Diana. It is in my nature to be pompous. But the Bread of Life fed me, and gradually I was emptied of that pompousness.

Lights fall to blackout on the platform. Main stage is illuminated.

Act I, Scene 4

Scripture references: John 6:1–13, 25–69

The shore of the Lake of Galilee. JESUS *stands upstage center, preaching to the people; however, the audience does not hear what he is saying. The* DISCIPLES *and the* CROWD *are around him, focusing their attention on him.* JUDAS *is upstage right. Near him are* YOUNG JOHN *and* PETER. ANDREW *and* PHILIP *stand downstage left, talking together.*

ANDREW *(looking out into the audience, as if searching for someone)*: Where *is* the lad? He should have been here at noonday.

PHILIP *(a little sarcastically)*: A little **hungry**, are we?

ANDREW *(quieting him)*: Sh-h-h-h! Do you want this whole hungry crowd to hear?

JONATHAN *enters downstage right, carrying a large basket full of food, and crosses to where* ANDREW *is.*

ANDREW: Where have you *been*, Jonathan? I've been worried …...

PHILIP *(poking fun)*: **And** hungry.

ANDREW *(giving* PHILIP *a dirty look)*: All right! All right! I'll share. Let's see what you have with you, my lad. *(He starts to look through the boy's basket.)*

JONATHAN *(chatting on, not even worried about anyone hearing)*: Mother was having trouble getting the bread to rise. She had to borrow some yeast from our neighbors. And then the oven wouldn't fire right. She sent me to fetch more wood from the roof …

ANDREW *(producing some fish and holding it up so the audience can see)*: By the prophets! That woman thought of everything! Smoked fish. Barley loaves—my favorite! *(handing one loaf to Philip)* Here … one for you and one for me.

JONATHAN *looks at him expectantly.*

ANDREW: Oh, all *right*, Jonathan! You can have half … of *Philip's* loaf.

As he says this, ANDREW *quickly takes back the loaf he has just handed* PHILIP, *which* PHILIP *has almost raised to his mouth. He quickly divides the loaf in half, giving part of it to* JONATHAN, *and then hands the rest back to* PHILIP. JONATHAN *receives it gratefully, while* PHILIP *looks at the depleted bread loaf with obvious disapproval.*

PHILIP *(less than gratefully)*: Many thanks, oh generous one!

They all start to eat the bread.

JESUS *(Separating Himself from the crowd, He comes over to where* PHILIP, ANDREW, *and* JONATHAN *are standing)*: Philip!

PHILIP *and* ANDREW *hurriedly hide the bread behind their backs.* JONATHAN, *oblivious to the problem presented by their selfishness, continues to eat his bread throughout the next exchange.*

JESUS: Where shall we buy bread for … *(indicates the other* DISCIPLES *and the* CROWD*)* … these people to eat?

PHILIP *(His mouth full of bread, he guiltily tries to swallow what he has in his mouth, but he cannot do it quickly enough to avoid talking with his mouth full.)*: Eight months' wages would not buy enough bread for each one to have a bite. Let's ask Judas.

He turns to ask JUDAS.

13

JESUS *(sternly)*: Do not ask someone else to do your work as a servant of God. *You* feed them.

PHILIP *and* ANDREW *look surprised and flustered.*

PHILIP: *Us?* We ...

ANDREW: Lord, I ...

JESUS *(looking at the basket)*: Show me what you have.

ANDREW *(brushing off the "absurd" idea that he share his food)*: Lord, the boy here has only five *small—very* small—barley loaves and two *tiny* fish! How far can that little bit go among so *many* people?

JESUS *(moving so He can look* JONATHAN *in the eye)*: And you, my young friend—what is your name?

JONATHAN *(very proudly, but not pompously)*: Jonathan, son of David, sir.

JESUS *(kindly)*: Well, Jonathan-son-of-David, how would you feel if I used the food in your basket to do the will of God the Father?

JONATHAN *(with innocent reasoning)*: Well, Mother says the food comes from God, so I suppose it still belongs to Him. *(pauses, hesitant to ask)* But can *I* have a piece of bread when God is done with it?

JESUS *laughs and tousles the boy's hair, pleased with the boy's answer.* PHILIP *and* ANDREW *look helplessly at each other.*

JESUS *(pointing to the basket* JONATHAN *has brought)*: Jonathan, you will use that very basket to gather up more than enough bread to feed your family this evening. Andrew, Philip ... *(calling other* DISCIPLES*)* John! Peter! Have everyone sit down.

YOUNG JOHN *and* PETER *come forward and do as he has just instructed them.* JESUS *takes some bread from the boy's basket and steps to downstage center.*

JESUS: Father, I give You thanks for bread and fish. I thank You for the people who served us by preparing this meal, that You may be glorified.

JESUS *breaks the loaf He is holding in half and gives half to* ANDREW *and half to* PHILIP. *He takes another loaf, breaks it, and hands half to* YOUNG JOHN *and half to* PETER.

JESUS: Feed the people.

ANDREW *and* PHILIP *hesitate for a few seconds, looking at* JESUS. *Then they join* YOUNG JOHN *and* PETER *in urging the people to form a circle. Once the circle is formed, all four* DISCIPLES *turn their backs to the audience, joining the circle downstage center. Meanwhile, another actor has secretly brought another basket inside the circle, filled with loaves of bread and some prop fish. Each person takes two loaves in his or her hands. On the silent count of three, the* DISCIPLES *and the* CROWD *turn toward* JESUS, *an amazed and pleased look on their faces, deliberately showing their bread and fish to the audience. The effect is that there is bread and fish everywhere, filling each person's hand.*

JESUS *(pleased and raising thankful hands toward Heaven)*: Gather anything left over. Let nothing be wasted.

All freeze. Lights fall to blackout on the main stage. Platform is illuminated.

Act I, Scene 5

Scripture references: John 6:13–15, 23–40, 48–58

JOHN THE ELDER *and* DIANA *resume their conversation from Scene 3. All characters from the previous scene exit quickly and quietly.*

JOHN THE ELDER: I remember that there were twelve baskets of leftover scraps. Little Jonathan was the happiest of helpers that day. The rest of us—all of those who had traveled with Jesus for over two years—felt too embarrassed to celebrate, too amazed to see Jesus' power used to feed hungry people while we tried to feed only ourselves.

DIANA: Why didn't Jesus proclaim Himself king then and there? *(making a fist and slamming it onto the table)* Such power could have been used to grind Rome into the dust!

JOHN THE ELDER *(looking hard at her)***:** There were many people who came to Jesus after that and told Him that was what He should do. *(Pause. Slowly, thoughtfully, he breaks off a piece of the bread sitting on the plate in front of him.)* But He responded, "I am the Bread of Life. He who comes to Me will never go hungry, and he who believes in Me will never be thirsty."

DIANA *(still skeptical)***:** What nonsense! He said He was **bread**?

JOHN THE ELDER *(Coming to an important point, he holds the bread up in front of him.)***:** Yes. He said, "I am the living bread that came down from heaven. If anyone eats of this bread, he will live forever. This bread is my flesh, which I give for the life of the world." *(He eats the piece of bread he has been holding.)*

DIANA *(jumping up)*: What madness is this? A man's flesh is **bread**? Did He mean we were to **munch** on Him ...like corn?

JOHN THE ELDER *(standing and looking into her eyes)*: He knew that the things we eat become a part of us. And the things that eat **us** make us into things we do not want to be.

DIANA *(sitting down and softening somewhat)*: Have you never been **angry**, old man? Have you never hated those who hurt you for no good reason? Have you never hated the Romans and the stupid crowds who cheer them, and the wealthy fools who supply them with horses?

JOHN THE ELDER *(simply)*: Yes, I have. I have hated. I once hated enough to kill. *(He sits.)*

Lights fall to blackout on the platform. Main stage is illuminated.

Act I, Scene 6

Scripture references: Luke 9:51–56; John 10:11–16

A road through Samaria. JESUS, YOUNG JOHN, JAMES, JUDAS, PETER, *and the other* DISCIPLES *are traveling toward a Samaritan village. One disciple carries a water bottle and ladle. They slowly walk up the church aisle toward the front of the stage or church.*

JAMES *(wearily)*: It will be good to rest in the next village. We must have traveled twenty-five miles today.

PETER *(grumbling)*: Twenty-seven, but who's counting?

YOUNG JOHN: I hope Andrew has found someone who will let us rest in their courtyard for the night, on some nice fresh straw. *(stopping to rub his back)* Sleeping in the fields may be *peaceful*, but rocks are hard and uncomfortable.

JESUS *(gently)*: Children, the hour is short. We must push on.

JAMES *(whining a little)*: Surely, Master …

ANDREW *enters from downstage right and stops everyone at the front of the stage.*

ANDREW *(breathless and afraid to tell them the bad news)*: Master, we cannot stop at the next village. They say they will not welcome You. They have heard You are going to the Passover feast at Jerusalem, and they are angry. They say they will *stone* us if we enter!

YOUNG JOHN *(angrily and self-righteously)*: *Stone* us, will they? We only come to give them the news of the Kingdom of God!

JESUS *(calmly)*: Their hearts are not ready. We cannot **make** them listen. *(pause)* Perhaps we should rest here for a while.

Most of the DISCIPLES *sit down with sighs of relief.* JAMES *and* YOUNG JOHN *take hold of* JESUS' *arms and lead him to downstage left.*

YOUNG JOHN *(beside himself with anger)*: Lord, do you want us to call fire down from Heaven to destroy them?

JESUS *(Disengaging from their grasp and turning so that He gazes fully into their faces, He speaks sharply.)*: No, James! No, John! You have no idea what kind of spirit has taken hold of your thoughts. The Son of Man has come as a **servant**, not as a **judge**. I tell you the truth: I am the Good Shepherd. The Good Shepherd lays down His life for the sheep. When they stray, He neither abandons them nor invokes the wrath of heaven down on them. I have sheep from other places that must come into the fold. It may take time, but they will come.

JESUS *moves to upstage center, where He finds the water bottle and prepares to serve the* DISCIPLES *a drink.*

JAMES *(still angry and smarting from the rebuke)*: The Master is not thinking clearly. Those Samaritans have insulted us, and they have insulted the God we serve.

YOUNG JOHN *(thoughtfully and rather penitently)*: Insulted **us**? Yes, they have done that. But perhaps we should wonder if **we** haven't insulted God ourselves.

JAMES *(dismissing what he is saying; angrily crossing to downstage right)*: The heat has affected your brain, brother! Should not the Master be given honor as the servant of the Almighty?

YOUNG JOHN *(taking his brother's arm and turning him to look at Jesus)*: If the Master has been so insulted, why is **He** so calm? He knows the mind of God better than anyone I've ever met. Why should **we** be angry if **He** is not?

JAMES *(still wishing to make a point)***:** Let me ask you …

JESUS: Come and help Me serve the brothers, will you, James?

JAMES *stops speaking and goes and helps* JESUS. YOUNG JOHN *remains downstage, thinking. All freeze. Lights fall to blackout on the main stage. Platform is illuminated.*

Act I, Scene 7

JOHN THE ELDER *and* DIANA *resume their conversation from Scene 5. All characters from the previous scene exit quickly and quietly.*

DIANA *(derisively)*: Your Master was a ***fool***! If He had the power of a king, why did He let those Samaritan dogs reject Him?

JOHN THE ELDER *(with understanding)*: If He had forced His way into the village and used His power to protect His disciples, what would have happened then?

DIANA *(angrily)*: Those swine would have learned a lesson they would never forget!

JOHN THE ELDER *(Pause. gently)*: Diana, how did you become a slave?

DIANA *(Shocked, she stands as if leaving.)*: I don't want to talk about it.

JOHN THE ELDER *(persistently)*: Was it a good experience?

DIANA *(answering sarcastically)*: No, it ***wasn't***! *(She spits at the ground.)* A curse on those who took me from my village!

JOHN THE ELDER: So you do not love your captors, or serve them willingly?

DIANA: Do I ***look*** like I love them? They are the scum of the earth!

JOHN THE ELDER: If Jesus wanted those Samaritans to love God, His Father, and to serve Him willingly, how would His invasion of the village have accomplished that? Would it be a joyful thing to them that He came? Would they then serve God with gladness in their hearts?

DIANA *(long pause)***:** You may have a point.

Lights fall to blackout on the platform. Main stage is illuminated.

Act II, Scene 1

Scripture reference: Mark 8:31–38

Jerusalem in the week before Passover. MARY MAGDALENE *and* PETER *enter from downstage left.*

PETER *(exuberantly)*: Is it not as I said it would be, Mary? The crowd's welcome! The roar of the people! *(He waves an imaginary palm branch.)* "Hosanna! Hosanna! Blessed is He Who comes in the name of the Lord! Hosanna!"

PETER *takes off his cloak and spreads it ceremonially on the floor, downstage center, imitating the actions of the crowd.*

MARY MAGDALENE *(too quietly)*: Impressive, Peter. Very impressive.

PETER *(stopping, puzzled)*: What's wrong? Were they not loud enough for you?

MARY MAGDALENE: *Too* loud. I fear a crowd that shouts instead of listens.

PETER *(still exuberant)*: This was a *time* to shout, Mary! They were shouting their joy; that's all.

MARY MAGDALENE: The priests—*they* were not shouting!

PETER: They fear the crowds. That is a good thing.

MARY MAGDALENE *(suddenly very earnest, clutching* PETER'S *arm)*: Do you not fear this, Peter? Do you not fear the power of the priests and the Sanhedrin?

PETER *(very confident and reassuring)***:** Mary! You **saw** how the people loved Jesus! They will not let anything happen to Him.

MARY MAGDALENE: And what will keep them—the crowd— happy, Peter? What will keep them on the Master's side?

PETER *(a little less confident)***:** Why, they will see ...

MARY MAGDALENE *(pursuing his thought)***:** See what?

PETER: His power ...

MARY MAGDALENE: ... Which He uses only to serve His Father.

PETER: His message ...

MARY MAGDALENE: ... Which so many in Galilee and Samaria have already rejected.

PETER: His miracles ...

MARY MAGDALENE: ... Which are only for those who see with the eyes of faith.

PETER: Mary, you worry needlessly.

MARY MAGDALENE: Peter, I worry **with good cause**. Did not the Master predict He would die at the hands of the authorities?

PETER *(with a certain bravado)***:** But I spoke to Him about that ...

There is a long pause as he remembers something embarrassing.

MARY MAGDALENE *(insistent)***:** And He said **what**, exactly?

PETER *(somewhat embarrassed)*: He said, "Get thee behind me, Satan! You do not have in mind the things of God, but the things of men." And then ... *(pause)*

MARY MAGDALENE *(encouraging him to finish his thought)*: Yes?

PETER *(uncomfortable)*: He reminded us yet again that those who would find this "new life" He teaches about must sacrifice their own desires, pick up the cross, and walk behind Him.

MARY MAGDALENE *(slowly and emphatically)*: Cross ... sacrifice ... not glory or honor.

All freeze. Lights fall to blackout on the main stage. Platform is illuminated.

Act II, Scene 2

Scripture reference: John 12:23–28

JOHN THE ELDER *and* DIANA *resume their conversation from Act I, Scene 7.*

JOHN THE ELDER *(reflectively)*: That last week of His earthly life went by so *fast*. We were all too blind to see where it was going to lead Him—to lead *us*.

DIANA: What a foolish leader to walk right into the hands of His enemies!

JOHN THE ELDER *(takes a moment to look at her)*: Foolish? Perhaps to some people. But He saw clearly what the Father wanted Him to accomplish, and He never turned His face away from that task.

DIANA: It would seem to me that His task was to stay alive and use His power.

JOHN THE ELDER *(slowly and dramatically)*: No, His task was to die.

DIANA *(pause in shock)*: Ridiculous!

JOHN THE ELDER *(pause)*: Diana, how did you make the bread this morning?

DIANA *(laughing)*: The same way I *always* make it!

JOHN THE ELDER: Did you make it out of nothing?

DIANA: Of course not! Has the night air mixed up your brain, you foolish old man?

JOHN THE ELDER: Then you made it *with* something?

DIANA *(hurriedly naming the ingredients)***:** Yes, yes … flour, yeast, water, oil …

JOHN THE ELDER *(interrupting her)***:** And the flour … it came from …

DIANA *(talking as if to a silly child)***:** *Wheat*, as if you didn't know.

JOHN THE ELDER *(in an insistent tone)***:** Is the wheat *alive*, Diana?

DIANA: It comes from a plant.

JOHN THE ELDER: And the plant … does it yet live? Does it yet grow and ripen?

DIANA *(making fun and explaining quickly)***:** No, you silly goose! The field hands harvested it, and then they beat it to separate the grain from the chaff, and then I ground the grain into flour.

JOHN THE ELDER *(pressing home his point)***:** Is it not *foolish* of the grain to give up its life so that we may have bread?

DIANA: I … *(She stops as the point he is trying to make dawns on her.)* This bread … the Bread of Life. He called Himself the Bread of Life. Is that how He meant it?

JOHN THE ELDER *(pause)***:** His physical life on earth had to come to an end in order to be Bread for our spiritual lives.

Lights fall to blackout on the platform. Main stage is illuminated.

27

Act II, Scene 3

Scripture reference: John 12:23–28

It is the day before the Passover in Jerusalem. JESUS, PETER, YOUNG JOHN, HELENA, SALOME, and the others enter from downstage left, talking softly among themselves. HELENA and SALOME stop downstage center. The others keep walking and exit downstage right.

HELENA: Salome, what *is* the matter with you?

SALOME *(very solemnly)*: It will come to a fight, I tell you.

HELENA *(puzzled)*: What *are* you talking about, my friend?

SALOME: Did you not see what those Roman soldiers did to that old woman at the gate just now?

HELENA *(resigned)*: I have seen many, many people pressed into service for Rome.

SALOME *(angrily)*: But to see a *mother* of Israel carrying their firewood like some slave!

HELENA: Salome, we are *all* slaves of Rome. Better to accept our state and make the best of life …

SALOME *(turning on her fiercely)*: The Master can *change* all that.

HELENA *(quietly)*: Yes, but does He *want* to change that?

JESUS reenters by Himself downstage right and listens quietly to what they are saying.

SALOME: Don't speak like that! The Master does not wish us to live under the fist of Rome! He is just waiting for the right moment.

HELENA: You are free to think what you wish, Salome. But I ask you: when has the Master spoken of rebellion? Where are the armies to fight for His cause? Where is the support of the priests and teachers of the law?

Salome is quiet.

JESUS *(walking toward the women)*: Salome, let me ask you ... what prevented **you** from helping the old woman with the firewood she was carrying?

SALOME *(startled)*: Master! I did not know You were there.

JESUS *(smiling)*: Your thoughts were plain as we walked through the city gate just now, my daughter. *(pause)* The hour has come for the Son of Man to be glorified. I tell you the truth, unless a grain of wheat falls to the ground and dies, it remains only a single seed. But if it dies, it produces many seeds. The man who loves his life will lose it, while the man who hates his life in this world will keep it for eternal life. Whoever serves Me must follow Me; and where I am, My servant also will be. My Father will honor the one who serves Me.... Follow Me.

He pauses to look into their eyes, and then JESUS *slowly turns and exits downstage right.* HELENA *and* SALOME *follow.*

Lights fall to blackout on the main stage. The platform is illuminated.

Act II, Scene 4

Scripture reference: John 14:1–3

JOHN THE ELDER *and* DIANA *resume their conversation from Scene 2.*

DIANA: Your Jesus was the strangest leader I have ever heard about—always talking about dying! Did He ever talk about *living*?

JOHN THE ELDER: He told us many times how to live *through* Him. And He told us how *He* would live again after He was crucified.

DIANA *(puzzled)*: Live *again*? Live on in your *thoughts*, perhaps …

JOHN THE ELDER *(insistent)*: No. He meant *alive* again—in His body—on this earth!

DIANA *(with deep skepticism)*: There is *no* life after death … *(She stands, picks up John's cross, looks at it, then throws it back down on the table.)* … and there is *no* coming down from a Roman cross to live again!

JOHN THE ELDER *(reassuring)*: How do you know, Diana? Have you ever been to paradise?

DIANA *(angrily)*: There *is no* paradise! There is only hell—and the fire of hatred that consumes us until we return to the dirt under our feet!

JOHN THE ELDER *(Standing, he puts his hand gently on her shoulder.)*: There *is* a paradise! Jesus went there—is there now—and He will someday welcome into paradise all of those who willingly become God's servants.

DIANA *(unexpectedly bursting into tears)*: If only I could believe you!

JOHN THE ELDER: You *can* believe me—not because *I* say so, but because *HE* said so, and He proved it with His own death and resurrection! *(He motions her to sit again.)* Let me tell you the rest of the story—how the Master died and how He came back to life again.

DIANA *slowly sits.* JOHN THE ELDER *also sits.*

Lights fall to blackout on the platform. Next scene is illuminated.

Act III, Scene 1

Scripture reference: Luke 22:7–13

A gate leading into Jerusalem. PETER *and* YOUNG JOHN *enter from downstage left. They are obviously looking for someone.* WOMEN *with watering jars are entering from downstage left and right, passing each other and staring at the two* DISCIPLES *as if they are out of place—which they are.*

YOUNG JOHN: Look—I don't want to be the one stuck with all the cooking, okay?

PETER *(speaking impatiently)*: Oh, now don't tell me **you're** going to prepare the unleavened bread, because if you think I'm going to let you sit around, watching the bread bake, you've got **another** think coming!

YOUNG JOHN *(trying to end what he's started)*: All right, all right … I'll split the chores down the middle! Now, what is it that we're supposed to be looking for, Peter?

PETER *(feeling foolish)*: A man carrying a water jar.

YOUNG JOHN *(repeating his words)*: A man carrying a water jar. Are you sure the Master said a **man**—**not** a woman?

PETER *(impatiently)*: What are you—an **echo**? *(He looks around him at the women passing by.)* There must be a **thousand** women carrying water to their homes to prepare for the Passover! How many **men** do you think will be doing **women's work** at this time of day?

YOUNG JOHN: I don't know. Maybe …

The MAN WITH WATER JAR *enters downstage right.* PETER *and* YOUNG JOHN *look at each other with surprise and then decide they ought to approach him. The* MAN WITH WATER JAR *walks to upstage center before* PETER *stops him.*

PETER (getting *him to stop*): Excuse me, sir!

MAN WITH WATER JAR (*pleasantly, but a little out of breath*): Yes? How can I help you?

PETER: Rabbi Jesus needs a room in which to celebrate the Passover feast with His disciples.

MAN WITH WATER JAR (*raising the jar so that he can carry it again*): We've been expecting you. Follow me.

YOUNG JOHN (*curious, reaching out to the man's shoulder*): Excuse me for asking, sir …

MAN WITH WATER JAR (*pausing, but obviously eager to get on with his task*]: Can't we talk as we walk? This water jar is rather heavy!

YOUNG JOHN: Exactly what I was going to ask about. Why are **you** doing the servant's work?

MAN WITH WATER JAR (*laughing with joy*): When my brother told me that Rabbi Jesus was to be a guest under our roof, I felt it was a privilege to serve Him.

YOUNG JOHN (*sheepishly*): Er, yes … you're right, of course.

The MAN WITH WATER JAR *leads* PETER *and* YOUNG JOHN *off, downstage left.*

Lights fall to blackout on scene. Resume illumination on main stage.

Act III, Scene 2

Scripture references: Luke 22:7–38; John 13:1–30

The Upper Room, in Jerusalem. A long table is stretched across the upper portion of the sanctuary. YOUNG JOHN *and* PETER *are busy placing dishes of food on the table.*

PETER *(very impatiently, to* JOHN*)***:** When are those unleavened loaves going to be done? The Master will be here any minute.

YOUNG JOHN *(equally impatient)***:** If *you* hadn't taken so long dressing the lamb …

YOUNG JOHN *produces a basin, pitcher, and towel from upstage left and proceeds with it to downstage right.*

PETER: Just remember … *I* get to sit by the Master's right side tonight!

YOUNG JOHN *(Having put the basin and pitcher down, he throws the towel down next to it.)***:** Now look here, Peter ! I'm sick and tired of you always pulling rank!

PETER *(boasting)***:** And just who is it the Master trusts with His closest confidences? Eh?

YOUNG JOHN *(pointing to himself)***:** Don't forget—my brother and I were *also* on the mountain when Moses and Elijah appeared with the Master! *We* heard the voice from Heaven as well! We are certainly as important as *you* are.

MATTHEW *enters down the center aisle.*

MATTHEW: Quit arguing, you two! The Master and the others are on their way. John, you'd better get ready to do the foot-washing.

JOHN *(shaking his head arrogantly)*: Oh, no! You're not saddling me with *that* job again!

PETER *(pulling rank)*: Now look here … you're the youngest! You *have* to do it—especially tonight!

JESUS *and the rest of the* DISCIPLES *enter from the rear of the sanctuary as* PETER *and* YOUNG JOHN *finish setting the table. The* DISCIPLES *are in a cheerful mood, while* JESUS *walks somberly. The* DISCIPLES *greet one another and take their places at the table, excluding the three arguing men.* JESUS *remains downstage right.*

YOUNG JOHN *(whining)*: Why can't one of *you* do it? I've been cooking hard all afternoon.

PETER *(quipping)*: You mean *burning* hard all afternoon!

PETER *and* MATTHEW *laugh.*

YOUNG JOHN: Go ahead … laugh!

While they argue, JESUS, *having reached downstage center, removes His cloak and tucks the towel that* YOUNG JOHN *has thrown down into His belt, like an apron. He positions the basin and pitcher downstage center.* YOUNG JOHN *is the first one He summons.* PETER AND MATTHEW *look on, dumbstruck.*

JESUS *(to* YOUNG JOHN*)*: Come, John. I must wash your feet first.

PETER *and* MATTHEW *move temporarily to upstage left.* YOUNG JOHN, *utterly embarrassed and glancing around at the others, slips off his sandals.* JESUS *then washes* YOUNG JOHN'S *feet and dries them with the towel.*

JESUS *(tenderly, to* YOUNG JOHN*)*: Do unto the others as I have done to you.

YOUNG JOHN *picks up his sandals and, ashamed, glances around at the other* DISCIPLES, *who are beginning to look sheepish, too.* YOUNG JOHN *returns to his place at the table.* JESUS *motions to* MATTHEW *and* JUDAS *that they are next.* JUDAS *looks very uncomfortable as* JESUS *washes his feet. After* JESUS *has finished with them,* PETER *approaches* JESUS, *as if to scold him.*

JESUS: It is your turn, Peter.

PETER *(blustering, reluctant to let* JESUS *touch his feet)*: Never, Lord. You will never serve me in this fashion.

JESUS *(straightening up to face* PETER, *with a serious warning in his voice)*: If I do not wash your feet, you can have no part in My ministry for God.

PETER *(obviously changing his* mind*)*: Master, don't stop with my feet! Wash my head and my heart as well!

JESUS *(smiles)*: A man who has taken a bath has no need to wash his whole body again. He has only to wash that part of him that has touched the dirt of the world, and he is acceptable. *(pause)* But not all of you are clean.

There is another pause, and a silence among the disciples. JESUS *continues with the rest of the people whose feet He needs to wash. When He has finished, He sets the basin, pitcher, and towel aside downstage right and puts on His own cloak. He speaks as He assumes His place upstage center at the table.*

JESUS: Do you understand what I have just done? I serve the Father in what I am about to do. You must serve one another. The love you show each other in willing service will be the beacon to the world. They will hate you because you display the purity of God's love to them. But you must take heart! I have overcome all the troubles of this world. *(JESUS looks at JUDAS)* One of you will betray Me shortly.

Each DISCIPLE *looks at another, puzzled, except for* JUDAS. *They buzz quietly with phrases like, "What does He mean?" and "Does He mean me?"* JUDAS *looks at the audience, as if to hide his face from the others.* JESUS *reaches for a piece of bread, which He then hands to* JUDAS.

JESUS: Judas, what you are about to do, do quickly.

JUDAS *holds the bread morsel for a moment, then throws it down and exits downstage left.* JESUS *takes a whole unleavened bread from the table and holds it for everyone to see.*

JESUS: I have eagerly desired to eat this Passover with you before I suffer. For I tell you, I will not eat this bread and drink this wine again until it finds fulfillment in the kingdom of God. *(He prays as He holds the bread up toward Heaven.)* Blessed are You, Lord God of the universe, because You have produced Bread for man. *(He divides the bread into two pieces and sends one piece to either side of the table.)* Take this and eat it. For this is My Body given for you. Do this to remember Me always.

(He picks up the cup and, holding it about chest level, pours wine into it from the pitcher on the table and blesses it.) Your bounty, oh Lord God, our King and our Father, has produced this Cup for mankind. *(He passes the cup to the right. As it follows around the table, each* DISCIPLE *drinks and looks at* JESUS.*)* Take and drink. This Cup is the new covenant in My blood, which is poured out for you.

*(*JESUS *goes to stand in front of the table. He is obviously very troubled in His Spirit.)* The hand of My betrayer has shared bread with Me! The Son of Man will go as it has been decreed, but woe to that man who has served another master in betraying Him!

YOUNG JOHN *(standing and coming to* JESUS' *side)*: Master, was it I? Was I foolish not to have done the foot-washing?

JESUS *(turning to them all)*: I say to you all: Do not be like the Gentiles. They love to exercise authority and to give themselves fancy titles. Instead, the greatest of you should be like *(He looks at* YOUNG JOHN.*)* the youngest ... and the one who rules like the one who serves.

YOUNG JOHN *starts to return to his place.* JESUS *looks at* PETER.

JESUS: Peter, I have earnestly prayed for you. Satan has asked permission to tempt all My disciples. But I have prayed for you, Peter, that your faith may not fail. When you have turned back from your own despair, serve your brothers; strengthen them as you have been strengthened.

PETER *(standing and approaching* JESUS, *thoroughly puzzled and boasting)*: What are you ***saying***, Master? I am ready this very minute to go to ***prison*** with you, even if it meant death.

JESUS *(laying a hand on his shoulder)*: Peter, before the morning cock crows, you will deny you ever ***knew*** Me.

Walking to stage right, JESUS *stares off into the audience, then He sighs and turns to the* DISCIPLES.

JESUS: Come. It is time to go.

The DISCIPLES *slowly follow* JESUS *out, downstage right.*

Lights fade out on scene. Resume illumination on main stage after all characters are in place for the next scene.

Act III, Scene 3

Scripture reference: Mark 14:32–52

The Garden of Gethsemane, after midnight. JESUS *is standing upstage center, praying. The* DISCIPLES *lie sleeping around him.* JOHN *and* PETER *lie downstage center. The lighting shifts between the Garden scene and the platform where* JOHN THE ELDER *and* DIANA *sit.*

JESUS *(earnestly; in pain)***:** Father! If it be possible—all things are possible with You—take this bitter cup away from Me!

Illumination shifts to platform.

JOHN THE ELDER *(remembering)***:** The first battle for the salvation of the world was won in a garden full of olive trees. Jesus knew exactly what lay in store for Him, and He was in great mental torment.

DIANA: Why did He not use His great power to defeat His enemies?

JOHN THE ELDER *(sadly)***:** He **did** use His power, but not to defeat the authorities. He used His power to overcome … *(with great emphasis)* ***Himself.***

Illumination shifts to garden scene.

JESUS *(showing submission)***:** Not My will, Father—only Yours.

Illumination shifts to platform.

DIANA: Did He battle with Himself for a long time that night?

JOHN THE ELDER *(guiltily)*: I don't really know. I was asleep.

DIANA *(mocking)*: You fell *asleep*? You did not serve your Master in what you say was one of His worst hours?

JOHN THE ELDER *(looking steadily at her)*: That's right. I was all talk and no action.

DIANA *(laughing)*: Some servant *you* turned out to be! Did He ever know you were so "loyal"?

JOHN THE ELDER *(with utter sadness)*: Oh, He knew … He knew everything.

Illumination shifts to garden scene.

JESUS *(Walking over to YOUNG JOHN, JESUS touches him on the shoulder.)*: John, My heart is so heavy. Will you not watch with Me just one short hour? *(Touching Peter)* Pray, Peter, that you do not fall into temptation.

YOUNG JOHN *(rousing temporarily from sleep and yawning)*: Whatever You say, Master.

YOUNG JOHN *falls asleep again right away. Disappointed,* JESUS *returns to upstage center and prays again.*

JESUS *(clasping his hands together more earnestly)*: **Father! Hear Me!** I cannot bear to be separated from Your Love! The cup that You ask Me to drink is full of the worst bitterness! *(Pause. JESUS unclasps his hands and raises them in an attitude of submission.)* Nevertheless, not **My** will, but **Thine** be done!

Illumination shifts to platform.

DIANA *(picking up the cross to stare at it)*: So He was all alone the night before He was crucified.

JOHN THE ELDER *(reaching out to touch it, too)*: Yes, He was. And it was as much my fault as it was the others'.

DIANA *(Putting down the cross, she stands where she is and looks out into the audience.)*: I wonder if my father felt as alone on the night before *his* crucifixion. I only heard about his death six months later.

JOHN THE ELDER *(Standing, he touches her shoulder, and she sits down again.)*: You had no chance to help your father. I had every chance to help my Master, and I didn't.

Illumination shifts to garden scene.

JESUS *(With resignation, He walks slowly downstage to John and Peter.)*: Sleep now and take your rest! The Son of Man is about to be betrayed into the hands of sinners. Here comes My betrayer!

JUDAS *and several* GUARDS *march down the center aisle.* JESUS *passively watches them come.* YOUNG JOHN *and* PETER *rouse themselves, as do the other sleepy* DISCIPLES. *They are very confused and do nothing while the rest of the scene plays out.*

JUDAS *(flamboyantly, but not smiling)*: Hail, Rabbi!

He embraces JESUS.

JESUS *(after JUDAS has finished his greeting)*: Judas, do you do this dirty deed with a sign of love?

JUDAS *(impatiently waving to the soldiers)*: This is the Man! Get on with your duty!

The DISCIPLES *stumble off stage right and left.* JESUS *is bound by the* GUARDS *and led away down the center aisle.* JUDAS *follows the soldiers.* JOHN THE ELDER *speaks.*

Illumination shifts to the platform.

JOHN THE ELDER *(It is almost as if he watches again as* JESUS *is led away. He stands, puts his hands to his eyes as if to blot out the sight, and then lowers them to stare straight ahead.)*: You asked me awhile ago if I ever hated, hated enough to kill. I hated Judas that night. I hated those guards. But most of all, I hated *myself.* They were leading off the One Who had been the guiding light of my life for three years ... One Whom I had come to love. But my love was not great enough to serve Him in this hour. And for that act of cowardice, I wanted to die. *(pause)* But I didn't. *(Sitting down, he looks at Diana.)* Because in one great moment of clarity, I began to see that though I failed Him once, I need not fail Him again.

DIANA *(turning away from him, uncomfortable with this new thought)*: Failure is failure! No one can change the past; no one can reclaim it. We live with our failures, and we die with our hatred.

JOHN THE ELDER *(solemnly)*: You are very wrong, Diana. That night, things that Jesus had been saying and doing for those three years we had walked together came back to me. Words about the Father's all-forgiving love. Miracles performed for wretched lepers. Prostitutes with hope for a change. All given by Jesus. It was all about having another chance! *(pause)* When I caught up with Peter, we headed back into the city.

Lights fall to blackout on the platform. Main stage is illuminated dimly.

Act III, Scene 4

Scripture reference: Mark 14:53–72

The courtyard of the High Priest. AMOS, WOMAN #1, WOMAN #2, *and several* GUARDS *are warming themselves by a "fire" downstage center.* YOUNG JOHN *and* PETER *enter downstage right, cautiously.*

PETER *(afraid, drawing his cloak up toward his face as if to hide)*: You do all the talking! You know these people better than I do.

YOUNG JOHN *(annoyed)*: Some leader *you* turned out to be!

YOUNG JOHN *approaches* AMOS.

YOUNG JOHN: Psst—Amos!

AMOS *comes over to* YOUNG JOHN *from the fire. They go upstage center to converse.* PETER *walks tentatively over toward the fire, trying to warm his hands.*

WOMAN #1 *(pointing at* PETER*)*: I recognize you! You were with Jesus of Nazareth a week ago, when the people made such a big fuss over Him!

PETER *(looking right and left, trying to cover up his face more)*: You must be mistaken, lady.

GUARD *(insistent, also pointing)*: You're one of those disciples of His!

PETER *(growling)*: You're **mistaken**, I tell you!

43

Elizabeth G. Honaker

WOMAN #2 *(coming over toward him to have a better look)*: Sure you are. Your very **accent** gives you away!

PETER *(exploding in anger at her)*: ***I tell you I've never even met the Man!***

A rooster crows once. PETER, *startled at the sound and at himself, looks toward the fire and then at* YOUNG JOHN, *then flees offstage right.* YOUNG JOHN, *surprised and scared, runs out after him.*

Short blackout.

Act III, Scene 5

Scripture references: Luke 23:32–49; John 19:25–30

Golgotha. Three crosses are silhouetted on a screen upstage center. A ROMAN SOLDIER *stands guard downstage left. The audience does not see people actually on the crosses. Each respective cross lights up from behind when the relative person speaks.* JOHN THE ELDER *walks slowly down from his platform and positions himself downstage center, staring at the cross.* DIANA *follows him, but stands downstage left until later in the scene.* MARY MAGDALENE *and* MOTHER MARY *walk down the center aisle, crying.* JOHN THE ELDER *turns and goes to embrace them, leading them back to the cross, where they stand for a few moments.*

JESUS *(center cross, crying out with a loud voice)*: Father, **forgive** them! They don't know what they are doing!

DIANA *(facing the audience, she wonders to herself)*: How could He **say** such a thing at a time like this? I would curse them with the wildest curses of Hades!

The CAPTAIN *marches crisply up the center aisle with three wooden boards in his hands. He hands the boards to the* ROMAN SOLDIER *downstage left.*

CAPTAIN: See that these criminal charges are nailed up on the crosses, soldier.

SOLDIER *(reading the three boards to the audience)*: Salinius— what a punk! Glad they finally nailed **him** where he can't hurt anyone! *(reads next board)* Hmm ... "King of the Jews." *(turns to the middle cross, bowing mockingly)* Well, your **majesty**! Hope your accommodations are to your liking!

The CAPTAIN *and the* SOLDIER *laugh at this joke. The soldier continues reading.*

SOLDIER: I see they finally caught that Demetrius fellow. *(yelling at the cross upstage right)* Stole one too many baubles, didn't you?

DIANA *(startled)*: Demetrius! *(She moves to touch* JOHN THE ELDER'S *arm.)* Demetrius was my *father's* name!

SALINIUS *(from stage left cross, sarcastically to* JESUS*)*: Hey, "king" Jesus—if you're so powerful, get us down off of these crosses, and we'll be your obedient servants … won't we, Demetrius?

DEMETRIUS *(from stage right cross, not mocking at all)*: Don't you even fear God, Salinius, just as we're about to meet Him? We both stole, and now we're payin' for it. But Jesus has done nothing to deserve this terrible sentence! *(to* JESUS*)* Jesus, I'm not a prayin' man, but if You could just spare me a thought when You reach Your kingdom …

JESUS: Friend, I tell you the truth: today—this very day—you will be with Me in paradise!

There is the sound of a thunderbolt. At the sound of the thunderbolt, DIANA *doubles over as if in pain. She turns toward the audience, straightens up, and reaches out as if to touch someone's face.*

DIANA: Demetrius! Father! Was that really *you* that day? Was John right when he remembered your name? Did you really ask that favor of someone you never knew? *(pause, crying)* Can I ask for paradise from a strange Rabbi from Palestine? Can I let go of all the hatred that's given me strength to fight?

JOHN THE ELDER *(Coming away from* MOTHER MARY *and* MARY MAGDALENE, *he steps up to where* DIANA *stands)*: If He had power to keep from hating as He hung from that cross—if He had the power to promise Heaven to a thief who deserved far less—if He had power to take away the sins of the world and banish them from God's sight, then He has the power to change your life, Diana. He has the power to change *any* life that's given over to His control!

DIANA *(crying in anguish)*: I don't *want* to lose control over my life! I want to *live*—I want to be *free*! *(She sobs.)*

JOHN THE ELDER *(taking her hand)*: Turn and look at the cross of your Savior, Diana!

DIANA *(shaking her head)*: My father! They took my father from me! I hate them for it!

JOHN THE ELDER: People take things from us and hurt us every day. They wanted to take Jesus' life away—but they couldn't.

DIANA *(puzzled)*: But I thought you said …

JOHN THE ELDER: He *gave* His life up! He offered His life to the Heavenly Father to satisfy the punishment for our sins. It is a very deep thing to understand, Diana. *(pause)* On that day, I, too, thought they had taken everything from me and that my life was under the control of my enemies. But Jesus knew my heart. *He* gave me a reason to go on that day.

JOHN THE ELDER *goes back to the side of* MOTHER MARY *and* MARY MAGDALENE.

JESUS *(speaking to* MOTHER MARY*)*: Woman, here is your son. *(speaking to* JOHN THE ELDER*)* Here is your mother.

(Pause) It is finished. Father, into Your hands I commit My Spirit.

DIANA *(facing the audience)*: There is nothing left but the burial.

JOHN THE ELDER *(going to her side and looking at the audience)*: There is nothing left except the empty tomb.

Lights fall to blackout on both the main stage and the platform. Illumination resumes slowly on the main stage once scenery is changed.

Act IV, Scene 1

Scripture references: Matthew 28:1–7; Mark 16:1–7; Luke 24:1–8; John 19:38–42

A representation of the tomb belonging to Joseph of Arimathea sits upstage center. As the stage lights slowly rise, one can see that the large stone covering the entrance has been rolled back, revealing a dark, empty space within the tomb. MOTHER MARY *and* MARY MAGDALENE *walk down the center aisle to approach the tomb. They are carrying funeral spices. They speak as they enter the stage lighting.*

MOTHER MARY *(kindly)*: Why don't you give me the spices you've been carrying, and turn back before someone sees you? You will be safer that way.

MARY MAGDALENE *(reaching downstage center, she turns toward the audience, refusing to give up what she is carrying)*: Did **He** worry about His safety? Did He, even one time, refuse to do good because it cost Him something?

MOTHER MARY *(catching up to* Mary Magdalene*)*: Mary, you offer such love! But there can be no fitting reward for your service.

MARY MAGDALENE: Mother, the mercy and the goodness of God through Jesus has been reward enough for a lifetime of service.

Heavenly tones are heard.

MARY MAGDALENE: Mother, do you hear that?

The area of the tomb lights up as the ANGEL *appears from upstage right. The women react with fright and amazement.*

Elizabeth G. Honaker

ANGEL *(walking toward the women, consolingly)*: Why do you seek the living among the dead? Jesus of Nazareth is not here; He has risen! Remember how He told you, while He was still with You in Galilee, "The Son of Man must be delivered into the hands of sinful men, be crucified, and on the third day be raised again." Be sure to tell His disciples, and especially Peter, that He will see you all again shortly.

The women hurry off downstage right. Appropriate Easter music or a projected picture of Christ's triumph can be displayed while the ANGEL raises hands in worship.

Lights fall to blackout on main stage. Platform is illuminated.

Act IV, Scene 2

The action continues from Scene 1. JOHN THE ELDER *is standing on the platform, lost in thought.* DIANA *sits quietly next to him, watching him.*

DIANA: I do not believe that He came back from death.

JOHN THE ELDER: He did. I saw Him.

DIANA: You gave in to your own grief. You pretended to yourself that He was never crucified, that it had all been a terrible dream.

JOHN THE ELDER *(Coming out of his thought world, he spreads his arms wide.)*: And just **what** am I doing here? Why do I suffer imprisonment sixty years after these events, if it is all a fantasy?

DIANA *(defensively)*: Deluded people have been known to follow deluded paths.

PETER *and* MARY MAGDALENE *enter downstage right and wait motionless downstage center.*

JOHN THE ELDER *(chuckles)*: Peter was exactly as you were, at first. When Mary Magdalene came running to tell us of her encounter with the angel, Peter said ...

Main stage is illuminated quickly.

Act IV, Scene 3

Scripture reference: John 20:1–9

The Upper Room. There is a bench downstage right. PETER and MARY MAGDALENE speak. There is no pause between the last word of JOHN THE ELDER and the first word of PETER.

PETER: Rubbish, I tell you! Nonsense! Your grief has made you crazy.

MARY MAGDALENE *(Trying to get him to listen, she grabs his arm.)*: But, Peter, I **saw** …

PETER *(wrenching himself free of her grasp and answering sarcastically)*: You saw a sunbeam—big deal! So the sun danced …

YOUNG JOHN *(entering from downstage right)*: I believe her.

PETER *(disgusted)*: Aw! Get away! (*He angrily turns and walks toward far left.*) You would believe **anything**, son of Zebedee!

YOUNG JOHN *(arguing)*: And you are like your father's namesake, Simon Peter, son of **Jonah**! Wasn't he the prophet who ran away from the Lord's voice? Do you want to hang yourself from guilt, like Judas did Friday? *(pause)* Are you so blinded by your sinful feelings that you would deny even the **possibility** that He has risen **now**?

PETER *(Stopping where he is, he turns back to look at YOUNG JOHN and speaks quietly.)*: I know I was no leader then. *(pause)* I will be a leader now. Come. We will go—just the two of us. Mary, stay here.

PETER *exits downstage right, and* YOUNG JOHN *follows.* MARY MAGDALENE *looks after them, then sits downstage right.*

Lights fall to blackout on the main stage. Platform is illuminated.

Act IV, Scene 4

Scripture references: John 1:4, 10–12; Hebrews 12:2

JOHN THE ELDER *and* DIANA *resume their conversation from Scene 2.*

DIANA *(sarcastically)*: How do the dead come back to life? Do they receive new blood to replace the blood they lost in their execution? Are their bruises gone, their wounds made whole? Do they have all their teeth?

JOHN THE ELDER: There is an essence—a soul—a spirit in each man and woman, given to us by Father God. That Essence departed from Jesus the day He was crucified, and it was called back to Him by the power of God the third day after His death. We saw Him that Sunday night, and I tell you: He *was* flesh and bone. He *ate* with us. He *talked*. We *touched* Him. He still had the marks the nails made in His flesh. *(joyously)* But His body held far more *power* after His resurrection than during His ministry among us. *(remembering)* He breathed His Spirit into us. We felt His peace. And six weeks later, we received an *unimaginable* holy boldness!

DIANA *(Standing, she gathers up the plate and cup she brought to* JOHN THE ELDER *in Act 1. Her tone is cold again.)*: All very nice, old man. But it takes more than *"holy boldness"* to get the chores done! And I'll bet Master Arius will *not* be happy that I sat here listening to your fool stories!

JOHN THE ELDER: I cannot convince you. *He* must convince you, just as He convinced me.

DIANA *(moving down the stairs, frightened)*: Do not call on any ghosts! *(Lights rise on main stage.)*

JOHN THE ELDER: The Lord of Life is no *ghost*.

He pauses. Then he picks up the scroll he was writing on at the beginning of the play and walks down the steps to reach DIANA.

JOHN THE ELDER: Please read what I have written.

DIANA *(She sets the dishes down and takes the scroll from his hand. She reads aloud.)*: "In Him was life, and that life was the light of men. He was in the world, and though the world was made through Him, the world did not recognize Him. He came to that which was His own, but His own did not receive Him. Yet to all who received Him, to those who believed in His name, He gave the right to become children of God … " *(very slowly putting the scroll down and looking fully at JOHN THE ELDER)* What must I do to have what Jesus offered?

JESUS enters from upstage right, garbed in clothing signifying His resurrection. There is a small stole over His right shoulder. Facing the audience, He extends His arms toward DIANA and JOHN THE ELDER, as if to encircle them in His love. The wounds in His hands are clearly visible.

JOHN THE ELDER *(very gently)*: Pray with me, Diana.

After a moment's hesitation, DIANA kneels downstage center and folds her hands in prayer. JOHN THE ELDER stands behind her, slightly stage left, hands on DIANA'S head. JESUS stands behind JOHN THE ELDER, slightly stage right, raising his right hand over DIANA'S head. JESUS also blesses JOHN THE ELDER with his left hand.

JOHN THE ELDER: Father, I cannot reveal the truth of my story to Diana. You must do that. She seeks Jesus, the Author and Finisher of our faith, the Beginning and the End, the Savior of the world. She repents of her sinfulness and asks in Jesus' name for a new life, a new start, and a new hope. Please grant our prayer. Amen.

DIANA *(echoing him tentatively)*: Amen.

JESUS *removes the stole that He has been carrying from His right shoulder and places it on* DIANA'S *right shoulder. She does not see* JESUS, *but she lifts her head and smiles, seemingly transformed by His touch. Lowering her hands, she stands up and thoughtfully echoes* JOHN'S *words.*

DIANA *(wonderingly)*: A new life! A new start! A new hope!

She turns and hugs JOHN THE ELDER.

JOHN THE ELDER *(happily)*: It's true, Diana. He made it all possible.

DIANA *(looking at her hands)*: They are still slave hands.

JOHN THE ELDER *(He steps forward and takes one of her hands in his own. He looks at it.)*: Your hands may belong to an earthly master, but your heart belongs to Jesus, the Servant of God. He can change everything about being a slave, if you follow in His footsteps.

DIANA fetches the dishes and returns to center stage.

DIANA *(tearfully, but with a smile)*: The dishes still have to be washed, old man!

JOHN THE ELDER *(gently taking them from her)*: Can we serve the Lord … together?

DIANA *(She motions as if she doesn't want him to take them, then slowly gives them to him with a smile)*: Don't drop them, old man.

JOHN THE ELDER *(chuckles, then pauses)*: Wait, my friend … *(He walks back up the stairs and retrieves the cross, then he goes back to DIANA'S side.)* Perhaps remembering how **HE** served will help **us** to serve better!

DIANA *takes the arm of JOHN THE ELDER as they walk down the center aisle.* JESUS *watches with satisfaction as they go.*

Lights fall to blackout.